# The Things

Poems

# Jeff Oaks

LILY POETRY REVIEW BOOKS

Copyright © 2022 by Jeff Oaks

Published by Lily Poetry Review Books
223 Winter Street
Whitman, MA 02382

https://lilypoetryreview.blog/

ISBN: 978-1-7365990-7-5

All rights reserved. Published in the United States by Lily Poetry Review Books. Library of Congress Control Number: 2021941653

Cover Painting: "The Things", Jeff Oaks

For Steve and Ted

There is a time when death is an event, an ad-venture, and as such mobilizes, interests, activates, tetanizes. And then it is another duration…
Roland Barthes, *Mourning Diary*

Three be the things I shall have till I die:
Laughter and hope and a sock in the eye.

Dorothy Parker, "Inventory"

## Contents

### 1/

| | |
|---|---|
| 1 | Driving Lesson |
| 2 | The Things |
| 3 | On the Black Dog |
| 4 | To Spring |
| 6 | The Visit |
| 7 | Late Stage |
| 8 | Rhubarb |
| 9 | How We Lived |
| 10 | What Is To Be Done With Silence |
| 11 | The Purple Robe |
| 12 | Sonnet for the Long Summer |
| 13 | The Allegheny River |
| 14 | Kissing the River |
| 15 | Changeling |
| 17 | The Telephones |
| 19 | The Shit |
| 20 | Small Rain |
| 21 | Water |
| 22 | Dallas That May |
| 23 | My Mother's Other Children |
| 24 | Threading Needles |
| 26 | The End of Summer |
| 27 | The Last Good Time |
| 29 | At the End of the Street |
| 30 | The End |
| 31 | Pomegranate |
| 32 | In the End Our Prayer Was |
| 33 | Being Met |
| 35 | The End, At Last |
| 36 | After Grief |

**2/**

| | |
|---|---|
| 39 | The Black Dog in the Middle of the Night |
| 41 | Going Back |
| 42 | What We Knew |
| 44 | Why They Drank |
| 45 | Lightning Mother |
| 47 | Lines Near Midnight |
| 48 | Lines at the Winter Solstice |
| 49 | Last Things |
| 50 | Tick |
| 51 | The North |
| 52 | From the Book of Durations |
| 53 | MotherBird |
| 54 | Lines After Waking |
| 55 | Begin (river) |
| 56 | Fable |
| 57 | Early Morning Rain |
| 59 | Begin (root song) |
| 60 | Lines Where Something was Supposed to Be |
| 61 | Begin (rain) |
| 62 | Pomegranate 2 |
| 63 | Talking to the Dead |
| 65 | Varieties of Green and Distance |
| 66 | Laughter Among Friends |
| 67 | Advice |
| 68 | Even in Pittsburgh |
| 69 | The Questions |
| 70 | Driving |
| 71 | When We Disappeared |
| 73 | Like Grass |
| 74 | "In my craft..." |
| 76 | *Acknowledgements* |

1/

Driving Lesson

The view was great     the little houses sat
close to water sunshine died in daily
and what a way to leave it     he thought
a shark's purse one day and nothing the next
the three dogs panted and the ocean kept coming
she ground her teeth against the painful work
of shifting gears     a broken hand     a twelve
year old     a garden full of upright flowers
the ancient clocks all told     of jars of pickles
of applesauce the man had smashed     the way they sparkled
wildly in thin moonlight     the wind arose     a parrot
somewhere else whistled uncle     all the arrow heads
he'd given me     Shift     she said     it was tricky

## The Things

We walk among her things, my mother pointing
to *That? How about this?* Frankly I nod
at everything: I'll take even the gesture
she makes, straight index finger, the middle, ring,
the little fingers curled under.  If I could.
Failing that, *any of these?* Yes, her figurine
toads, pelicans, a snail, a pair of blue parakeets,
even the slim cabinet. Bought over the years.
Even though I hate to dust.  Yes to her books
unless my brother wants to keep them.  Yes
to the bed she can't sleep in anymore, the pots
and pans she can't lift, the sheets, the chairs.
She keeps pointing at her estate without
any sign of remorse or regret.  *I won't mind not
vacuuming when I'm gone.  Remember that.*

On the Black Dog

All my clothes were already dark.
It was the same summer my mother was
diagnosed with stage four lung cancer in her liver.
I wept standing up. Sometimes for so long
I thought I might disappear. I needed the leash,
the green park, something to do with my voice
that didn't hurt, the comfort of warm fur at night,
even the hot heavy stink I learned to grab, tie off,
and throw away every morning which became,
in the midst of everything, nothing, a habit, a life.

## To Spring

Every day I walk the dog beside the river
twice. Every day whether the river is green
or blue or brown, whether it's high or low.
Every day whether there are herons or geese
or only the sound of river ice grinding
against shore ice, a sizzle that shivers
ice shards like flames around the seam.
Every day I come back home and drink
water out of a large white mug
I bought in a hardware store one day
near Hampstead Heath right after I'd seen
Keats' house with its propped-up ancient
plum tree outside, his death-mask, the hand-
written copy of "O Bright Star" in his Shakespeare.
The truth is I went there because, except for
"To Autumn," I hadn't liked him much and
hoped seeing his house would light
a little sympathy in me for all his sighing
and moaning, all the strange men groaning
about nightingales and old jars, dead knights
and distant girls. I think buying the large
plain white mug was my response. I wanted
something simple out of which to drink clear water.
It might have been something Keats never
got to do, I think now. God knows what
had to be done then to get to clean water,
nevermind the clear, the simple. He came to
his simplicity late for my taste, but
sometimes I too feel *o'erbrimmed* watching
the Allegheny push its tonnages downstream,
a mix of branches, mud, poison ivy,
a wood duck slipping out of its manmade box,
the kids tagging their names in spray paint
on the gigantic pillars of the 40th Street Bridge.

It flashes past. Life flashed past Keats
and all that crew listening to their teeth rot
and their breathing grow pock-marked, bloody
as Indian Paintbrush. Here near the river
grow large purple clover bumblebees grapple
like adolescents at nipples. Once
by accident—not truth or beauty—I found
enough morels to fill a doggy bag.
I took them home and washed them
until they were the color of the moon.
Then I sliced them in half and in butter,
fried them. I ate them happily.
I washed their sweet flesh down
with clear water from that plain mug
I bought for almost nothing elsewhere.
I told no one. Who else did I need?

## The Visit

The oxygen machine trembles, clicks, hisses.
Through clear green tubes running into
the bedroom, up to her face. I hope
she's fallen back to sleep without me there
snoring in her old bed while she's nearby
in the electric hospital one that raises and lowers.
To leave her alone, I've come into the living room
and cranked back her recliner.
I can see what a pain the living are.
Even these hyacinths my brother bought
for her eightieth birthday are a burden.
They can't hold their perfumey heads up.
She asked me, *"What do you know about bulbs?*
*Can I just wrap up the bulbs and give them to you?*
*Or do the flowers have to die to make a new one?"*
Engine and catch of breath. Sentence. Meaning.

Late Stage

"Flourish and ruin keep leaving each other,"
wrote Liu Tsung-yuan around 800 A.D.
But frankly this is about my mother.

He was in exile, mourning another good government
sunk by aristocracy.

"Flourish and ruin keep leaving each other,"
he wrote to an old friend, meaning, don't suffer;
nothing stays lost. Of the pine tree they
planted together, he wrote, "cold

blossoms its kingfisher-green."
It was a beautiful solace clearly.

"Flourish and ruin keep leaving each other,"
so nothing was safe. "The bloom of youth scatters.
Grandeur crumbles." But the tree had a "radiant beauty"
which has everything to do with my mother.

Things always live between states. Some prosper.
At the end, the poet wanted "just clear wind for company."
Because flourish and ruin keep leaving each other.
How could this not be about my mother?

## Rhubarb

All along every fence we owned the smoke
of its dark green leaves rose. It choked out
everything else except the cats who took
to vanishing under its poisonous umbrellas.

At the edge of what we owned, the edge
of every garden where summer Sundays my father,
shirtless, sweated himself sober, baked himself red,
among tomatoes and peppers, half-alive, half-dead.

Not everyone could eat those stalks raw the way
my family did, like a kind of erotic celery grown
bloody in the shade they shared with harvestmen.
If a thing didn't hurt, it wasn't anything then.

We watched it growing. Like I said,
we ate it. We thought it tasted good.

How We Lived

Again and again we drove into the night
to find a place where no one could find us.
Over and over we parked in darkness,
practiced being nothing but breathing, fog
on the windows instead of our faces.
We sat sometimes a long time, listening.
Our two dogs in the backseat settled
into waiting. One night something was wrong
with my mother's right elbow; another night
something kept her hand from making
a fist, something gone rose-colored, a throbbing pain
she kept to herself. Some nights when
her left hand let loose the steering wheel
its knuckles were snow. When she opened the door,
the domelight was a headache, another slap.
I opened my door; the seatbelt reeled back
its elastic. We were no one to know,
we hoped no one would see us check in
for one night, with two dogs and no tent.
How we signed in, her with a broken hand,
bruises on her arm, unable to write,
I don't remember. No one asked.
Somebody always took our money
and let us stay in a spot where a family's
supposed to go. Instead, we unfolded
the backseat into a bed, climbed in, and slept.
The dogs folded themselves around us.
In the morning we drove back
to the house we escaped. I shifted
the stick when she said *Now,* heard her
grunt of pain around each lurch. *Remember what
we've had to do,* she said when her breath
returned. *Remember all of this.*

## What Is To Be Done with Silence

On one hand, it's death.
On another, there's breath
regained in it. Ears unring in it.
Some days go on in it
in perfect happiness.

                        The dog
lies down in it, sighs out
what barks he has left in it.
A few minutes later, asleep,
his tail begins to beat the air.

My mother made plans in it
to leave and start again in it,
where silence might not be another
waiting to be hit. (The slow
sizzle of her picking herself
off the floor in it while he sat down
and wept without apology.)

Much of the country lives lives in it,
without one friend to trust
or turn to. Minute by hour by
day of it. Filling the ticks
of the terrible old clocks
we had to remember to wind.

The lucky ones find books
in it, become filled with it,
such spaces in it in which
to practice acting, learning
ways to live.
              Until they
can make a break from it.

The Purple Robe

Hers is inside-out, I realize, when she gets up
out of her recliner at 7 am. The pocket at her right hip's
flipped out like an ear. All the hairy stitches
show. *Do you know your robe is inside out?*
I say to her back, as she bends to turn off her oxygen flow.
She has a cane in one hand. She's trailing
a complicated tubing that curls and loops behind,
catching occasionally on chair legs,
on my left-out shoes. *I can't be bothered*
*with clothes*, she says. The last word's
barely a wheeze. She limps into the bathroom.
Mother of buttons, zippers, patches, bleeding
redblue threads around the seams.

Sonnet for the Long Summer

The Shattered Teeth Nightmare. My Jaw
Falls Out Nightmare. The Sudden White Face
At the Midnight Bedroom Window Nightmare.
The Sharks Circling Under the Leaking Boat

Nightmare. The Clawing Behind the Only
Door Nightmare. The Favorite Dog Running Out
into Traffic Nightmare. The Falling Out Hair
Nightmare. The Trapped Under the House

as It Falls Nightmare. The Showing Up
Unprepared to My Audition Nightmare.
The Rooms of Spiders. The Tickle That Turns Out
to Be a Floor of Snakes, Ankle-deep, Nightmare.
The Nightmare Where I Say *Goodbye, Mother*.
The Nightmare Where I Can't Breathe the Water.

## The Allegheny River

To stand near a river and feel the great slippery weight
sliding past like one of those long continuous trains from childhood
you watched go on forever, waiting in a car
with one parent or the other sighing, tapping fingers
on the outside of the car door. The enormous water which
begins as threads, a luminescent rustle among pine needles
against old granite, which wind themselves together, falling toward
the lowest places it can find. Your mother dead now.
Mine soon to follow. Then suddenly another friend's mother gone.
The first poet I read who wasn't dead is now dead.
And I'm standing by the river watching it move on.
The dog is fetching the sticks I throw into it. He's just
learned how to swim, and now he comes out of the fat water
and spins his skin first one way and then another,
flinging water the way I used to dream porcupines might
spray their quills. To stand and just watch it
move, slide, press on, all the weight of water,
without choice, without a thought for what goes into it,
or where it goes or what comes out again. To throw
a stick back into it for the dog to rescue.

## Kissing the River

A friend reminds me kissing the dog
means kissing the river, which she knows
is full of things I wouldn't ordinarily touch.

And I suppose she's right. I don't know
anything about what's in the water.
I only see my dog come running out of it,

his black tail wagging around him like a sprinkler
in wild circles, the pleasure he gets
shifting and shaking his skin, and it's hard not to

put my lips against his dark head,
as it's always been difficult not to put my mouth
to anything I want to keep forever.

## Changeling

There was a perfume like starlight,
which made her a starlet in that town
of mechanics. I stole a silver ring.
And the big red lipstick. When I
put them back, I was exact. No one
could have known. The streets
around us were brick or cobblestone.
Her clasp earrings hurt too much, the bracelets
slid around. There was one necklace
but she always wore it. I'm writing this
to explain why I took a knife and sliced
an X in my mother's jewelry box,
the one nice thing in an otherwise house.
It was clear my mother stood for something,
her perfume sharp and sweet, the smell of cold,
the middle of November, leaffall.
She was my magnetic north, wind blowing in
from the ends of the earth. Everything
about me was considered easy to watch.
The sitters lay on the couch and imagined
I was up to nothing in the mirror
reciting Antares, Arcturus, Centauri Prime.
When it came to light I'd been in
her jewelry box—I was the only one—
she said no more. I can't explain
where the knife came from, but
it was there. It was someone's.
Who would ever hear of the knife
otherwise? The breeze of the ocean
when they said goodbye for the evening,
all dressed up like the king and queen
of Saturn. I mean, who was I? I couldn't even

look another person in the face without
flinching. The knife might have been
a Swiss Army knife. I was always
expected to succeed. Even my sign
was an X, a mark a prisoner makes:
I was here. When they came home,
I stood, just outside her room
listening for her gasp, like a ghost,
her surprise late in life, a mistake,
with a full head of wild hair.

The Old Telephones

Some were square like the heads of Labrador Retrievers. The furniture then had to be heavy enough to support them. Each phone weighed the same as a full grown man or a woman in labor. Its ring alone could break dishes left out to dry. Those dark anchors we had to heft, black as a nun's bed or a gun's chamber just before the click. Only some of us were strong enough to lift those black barbells up to our ears. Remember, this was when we used to take baths only once in a while, when Dial soap might last months on the shelf. Called a cake then, it was your reward for swearing certain oaths. The water we bathed in came out of what we called a cistern, a stone vault below the house where rain collected and was redirected by lead pipes upward. When you got bored counting birds you could go down and watch shards of light slowly circle in it, water without wind, sometimes so quietly you might mistake its being full as being empty. We washed in that, yes, left what was warm sometimes for somebody else. If you were lucky, no one else walked in on you to say there was still more work to do, mowing the enormous lawn, cleaning the side windows. When those phones rang, you could hear them way out in the pear trees, way out near the blackberried fences where the trains blew warnings, loud and smoky, as if the telephone had conjured them as it could the firetruck, the ambulance, the police, the hearse's silence. Sometimes you could, if you did it very lightly, lift up the receiver from its cradle and hear one neighbor complain about another, which meant you could be overheard too. Black radio, black toad waiting to sing, part cast-iron skillet, part oven, it demanded we stay put, sit, when we talked to one another. Our ears hurt after awhile. To call out, we stuck our fingers into it and dialed until we heard it click, then a ring on the other side. In the winter, if the power went out, sometimes we had to dial in the dark and pray. We didn't always know then what we were calling people away from so we had to have something to say. People had things to do everyday. If phones rang at night, you knew it was death, and you hesitated before saying hello. Black thundercloud, bear waiting asleep in the cave. You might swear on one in the absence of a Bible. Those were the days we killed oxen and roasted them whole in pits. Big chunks of charred meat came piled on a platter and you ate it. You ate and you ate and you ate those days. You had to be strong because everything was made for the strong. This was when there was wilderness you could still get lost in. We had little choice: everything was either black or metal. Satellites watched us. Sometimes people called you just so you could hear them breathe.

The Shit

"I called because of the tornadoes," I say.
"I was worried about your power
cutting out and you unable to breathe."
*Everything's fine,* she says. *Except*

*I shat myself today. I can't believe it.*
"Well, if a tornado were screaming toward me,"
I say, "I'd shit myself too." Which makes
her laugh and lose her breath. *It's*

*too much of [medicine X]. Thank god
I can still get into the shower by myself!
But now I've got a shitty bathtub,
towels, shitty laundry.* "You already

had a shitty disposition," I say.
"Now you've got everything to match."
Again, that crackling, staticky laughter,
as if we were passing under a bridge,

driving through a tunnel, her air
turning to cellophane. *I can't wait
until you come down here again,*
she cracks. *I need to punch you.*

"Soon, soon," I promise. She says, *The sky's as black
as night right now in middle of the afternoon.*
"You're shitting me." *I shit you not.* "That's shitty."
*Pretty shitty,* she says, *in fact. A real shitstorm.*

## Small Rain

Morning tea black as an eye.
Dark taste runs through me
like a snake like a root.

What else in the birdsong
beside the birdsong? On the radio
some scientists have found

evidence for the particle
that brings mass to everything.
Another scientist says there's always

the possibility this will make us
all disappear in a microsecond.
Light rain today, cool breeze

moving through the house.
The carpenter bees in the eaves
will cost us something.

There's a window frame rotting
that needs repair. Another
celebrity couple is breaking up.

The black dog goes into the tiger lilies
in the back yard and takes a dump.
There are some things I don't have to

clean up for anyone other than myself.
Teacup in which I stare back at myself.
The sound of fans inside the house

like a constant rain falling
when in fact there's almost
no real rain coming down.

Water

Water we cross over.  Water we forget.  Water
we throw on fire without regret.  Water we step into.
Water we skip stones over.  Water we make steam.
Water hard as salt.  Water slipping blades between
slabs of sandstone, shale, and slate.  Water you
are made of, Mother.  Water of little, littler, less.
Water wash away.  Water in the gutters, in the eaves.
The swan in the mirror, the rain in the news.
All night we sleep inside it like stowaways.

## Dallas That May

No mountain in sight. One uninterrupted flat
earth over which the city spreads
like spilled mercury; even the lawns
glow uranium green as the fantails
of sprinklers lash over them one way
then another. In a month, everything will be dead.
Until then, these easy Newtonian rainbows
of the upper middle class. By July
an unbreathable heat will become confused
with God, which my mother, knowing the end
is coming soon, still refuses. Across the lawns,
boat-tailed grackles strut, beaks open,
feathers iridescent as gas. They practice
their rusty-hinged calls over the immigrant grasses.
Enormous vehicles wait in every parking space,
bunker after bunker, each a form of disbelief.
Vultures glide over the whole blistered place.
Making out of unbearable heat an unflappable grace.

## My Mother's Other Children

The first of us has no name
I know, only miscarriage, heartbreak.

In that shadow my brother grew
for eleven years, an only child.

Then I came, the late mistake.
When I asked why, she said

*I still had love to give.* Which I believed.
But one last child my mother conceived

out of my refusals to obey her.
*Don't you worry*, she'd say,

holding my plate of uneaten food,
*I'll just give this to Timmy. He'll eat it.*

*He loves me.* Then she'd wait a minute,
until, full of anger, I'd finish it. Already

I was waking up to their midnight fights,
walking downstairs and yelling *Stop*,

standing between my drunken father
at the table and her in the kitchen.

My older brother, having put in his time,
left as soon as he was able. Timmy of course

disappeared even sooner, being, as he'd been,
a thing without bones or compassion,

a real bastard,
leaving everything to me.

Threading Needles

*I wish you hadn't told me*
        my mother said as we were handing
each other needle and thread
        and trying to pass one through

the other, *about the Huntsman Spider*
        *being here now instead of over*
*there in Australia. I'll have*
        *nightmares about that.* She wet the end

of the thread with her lips as a way
        to sharpen and steady it. I looked
at the eye of the needle in the light
        and tried to poke the thread through it.

(At least as big as a tarantula
        and able to walk on walls and ceilings
and able if it jumps on you to cling
        against your attempts to shake it off,

I'd said.) *Sorry, it's just that*
        *I've gotten so used to telling you things*
*that it's hard to remember you're*
        *almost out of here.* Both of us

squinting to see. *These needles*
        she said *are supposed to be easy*
*to thread. But I'll be damned if I can.*
        Both of us trembling as we tried to keep

both arrow and target still enough.
        The way it came to me finally was
to point the narrowed thread upwards
        and bring the needle down on it.

*Ta da!* I said as I pulled the thread through.
    She said *You got it! Jesus, another*
*thing I've learned too late. Now please*
    *double-knot it just to be safe.*

## The End of Summer

Suddenly that great sadness of coats.
The echinacea turning pale, ragged
around their burnt pincushion centers.
The edges of the tickweed blacken and curl.
Suddenly, it seems, the large-headed sunflowers
stoop like Abraham Lincoln near the end of the war.
Stare at my feet. Inside the house,
the five white boxes my mother sent
of things I said I'd wanted, which
I'll have to make room for now, and which
she was glad to hear had arrived safely.
Somewhere among my container garden pots,
the one praying mantis who made it through
will appear soon, as I'm watering things
out of habit one cool morning. Suddenly
race toward me like a strange horse.

## The Last Good Time

She was so glad I'd come; there was
so much to be done; where did I want to eat?

She had a refund check to cash. She
needed to buy groceries. She

thought maybe that noodle place I like.
Her apartment complex shook with work.

There'd been a big storm, maybe a tornado
and now men up on the roof yelling,

their drills farting loud enough to make us laugh.
Someone fired a nail gun right over our heads.

*I half expect a foot to break through*,
she said. But none ever did.

At the Thai place, we ate curry and chocolate cake
and laughed at the food that fell on her breasts.

She smiled too long at a little boy eating nearby.
At the grocery store we wheeled around

inspecting manager's specials for a deal.
We cashed that check. It was almost normal.

For a while there was nothing better than
her life in Dallas, Texas, despite the awful traffic.

Only once, out in a parking lot did she stop still,
shrill pain in her left leg like lightning.

*The cancer in the bones* she said.
Her hand trembled in my hand.

Do you want to go home, I asked.
She almost sang. I recognized the sound

just before I want to scream.
*No, I just need*

*a minute. It gets bad but I want
to get things done.* And we did. Every bit.

We brought back bags of groceries she put away
when I went to check her mail. The men

were still ripping up everything, yelling down
for tools, for ladders. Some were crouched

in shadows drinking water, looking burnt.
When something boomed overhead, she said

*They'll be at it for days.* I vacuumed the rugs
she was unable to. At the end of the afternoon,

from the next building's roof, a man's long shadow
threw itself into the living room.

## At the End of the Street
*For Geeta*

In the old parking lot.  Where there's enough
darkness and distance to be struck by
the night sky: Venus' bright star
just above the moon's thin cupped crescent,
Jupiter beside them, a small red
irritation. Millions of miles away
and in opposite directions from us.
What were we saying just the other day?
Whatever annihilates you and leaves you
still alive, leaves you with the responsibility
to bear witness. To say Venus, Jupiter, the Moon,
even when you're completely alone.
We were talking about our parents dying then,
the grief of orphans hanging over us.

## The End

After the definitions of mercy
are murdered, after the forks
removed, after the furniture
has been turned to face the future.
After the last toad has been
silenced, after the imaginable
violence of this machine or the next,
after the robot on the help line
admits it cannot help, please
try again later when another
robot will be working; after
the sickness has begun burning
your photographs; after the old
translations were finally revealed
to contain an unpronounceable stretch
of water neither flood nor river
nor trickle nor drought. After
the drought and its angry Protestants,
its brittle owls afraid to call out,
the quick mice and grass long since fallen
into a fine quiet rust. After the rain
reappeared and started shouting
from the porch about the lack
of love, the new Moon, the lost Stars.
After the last joke about the last
two priests going into the last straight bar
only to find the last lawyer there
already drunk and with the last
altar boy under his arm. After an armadillo
enters, says the punch line and explodes.
After the hush. After the last mask is ash.
Even after that. We will never get there.

Pomegranate

As if a palace were behind each doorknob.
Underneath, among skin grafts, lost receipts,
rooms of ruby teeth, sweet kernels, glittered slippers.
Not a word about the underworld,

the buried bodies, decisions within decisions.
Where it flowered in a hiss of breeze and bees
the pomegranate's last desperate kiss prickles.
Listening to voices in another room,

turn one way or the other, ear against
the paper-thin wall, hand grown numb
from leaning on it all night, a patience

that unfolds, a flame from a scratch, the screech
owl opening its catcher's mitts of hooks.
Was a breath. Then nothing.

## In the End Our Prayer Was

To something small, where smell
ruled maybe. We'd killed all
the big things by then. What
was left to live by? What wanted
no sacrifice of what we had?
Among insects, desert plants.
Something patient, without fear.
Outside language. Beyond chance.
Which cut down will reappear.

## Being Met

If a gate. If a train. Whatever,
I am grateful for it. If a god.
If a dream or just imagined.
I'll close my eyes some day.
Out of tired. Out of strength
like tonight sick and out of breath.
Whatever. Really, whatever.
There's only so much. Maybe
one bag, an overnight. Something
light with all I remember missing
and all I remember of hope
tucked in my pocket like a ticket.
If a plane. If a boat. At the time
the transport comes. Whatever
the mind most wants to take.
I've taken every kind and been
grateful. Just a step up
and out and if there's luck
like my mother had, loved ones
there to meet you. She smiled,
they said, suddenly. If the morphine
at that point. If against all odds
a heaven or another side, all right.
She'd been loved. She didn't
mind dreaming of it again. If
there was rain. If your name's called.
Being taken somewhere else,
outside. If there were friends.
If angels. An old dog leaping up
again. I take my thick medicine
in the middle of the night and close
my eyes. It tastes like fuel. A kind
of current's in it, a kind of trance.
I feel my feet grow warm. If all

could be well when I wake.
If she thought that at last. Meanwhile
let her take one last ride
once again out to see the old place.
If an engine. If a crowd surrounds.
The whistle. The empty platform.

The End, at Last

In this case, my mother's voice disappears
after eighty years. Where has it gone? One
says heaven. One says everywhere. Someone
who loves me says Nobody knows. Meanwhile,
noisy construction has begun down the street,
removing the quiet abandonment
of the grassy lot where I always walked my dogs.

Soon, a hundred doors will open there,
instead of the complicated mix
of weeds, doorknobs, doorbells,
mailboxes, telephones, human grief
and joy. Car horns and bike chimes.
It's hard for me not to hate it.

## After Grief

There's an end to waiting but not right yet.
Let me sit here in the quiet a little bit more,
waiting for something other than breath
to move inside me, other than hunger,

other than thirst. There will be an end
but first I need to wait. Eventually I will
get up from here and begin, get dressed,
make breakfast, take the dog out, get to work.

It won't take long but for now I need to stay
quiet like a tourist listening for new sounds
outside the window, inside my own mind,

finding myself in a strange bed and slowly
reciting to myself the few words I know
in the strange language I will have to use.

2/

## The Black Dog in the Middle of the Night

Sometimes the black dog wakes you up in the middle of the night.
Sometimes the dog is Anubis.  Sometimes he's just your dog.
Sometimes you know something's wrong; there's
a terrible retching sound at the end of the bed.  Sometimes
you just feel him looking at you, a physical thing
like a voice, and you say his name in the darkness.
Because in the old days there was a dark god who came
to guide you down to the place of judgment. There,
your heart would be weighed against an ostrich feather,
on the scales of the law in the kingdom of death.
Anubis the guardian of the dead and of orphans.
Anubis son of the sea and the underground.
Anubis the last face you see if your heart weighs
more than the law, before you are devoured
by Ammit, who bursts, sometimes as a crocodile,
sometimes as a hippo, whatever you fear most,
out of hell's burning lake. The house is dark
and there is no noise from the street. You still
have not fixed that broken stair but you know how to
step over it by now. You remember where the leash was
and sure enough there it is again.  A tail bangs into you.
It's your dog, and not Anubis. You still have not
oiled the hinges on the front door. It's hard
not to think it must sound to the neighbors
like a man coming out of a tomb. The dog
pulls you down to the abandoned lot where
soon new foundations will be dug, upon which
new houses are planned for the well-off.
The black dog walks out into the new March grass
and pisses there.  You look at the stars,
find the two planets in the news, forget which is which,
burning brightly as if in love.  Not a single car
drives by. You think, well, if this is my
last walk I think I've done good work in the world;
I haven't damaged anyone intentionally.
The black dogs I've lived with, if I'm asked

for witnesses, would not turn against me.
Then a car passes, and whatever death it was
you were preparing yourself for lifts. The dog
just wanted to pee, you say to yourself, get
a grip, stop being so willing to die, good god
aren't you a strange one? The hinges
on the front door sound old and you think
tomorrow I'll finally go to the store and buy
some WD40 and make that creak disappear.
In the dark house, you find the treats on the counter
and give one to the dog who eats it fast.  He's hungrier
than you expected; it may be why he woke you up.
He knows the ritual of the dog who deserves
to be given something good in the night.
Quickly after, he jumps back onto the bed
and his breathing slows. Leaving you to stare
out at the quiet neighborhood, wondering
where your need to self-mythologize has led.

Going Back

The lake is still there, blue and deep.
The town still seems unable to get up.
They straightened the streets since
I was here last, corrected curves
I just managed to survive
when I was learning to drive. Or maybe
they took away the trees. Or the trees
died. The lawns all show signs of drought.

Driving north, toward an old friend's house,
I can feel where the state reduced the hills on
the old rural route we used to take because you could—
by gunning the engine just right—get enough lift to leave
your stomach behind. Someone hauled
those hills away somewhere. Probably to fill in
some swamp I used to think was beautiful.

## What We Knew

Every time my cousin Paul made jokes about how
we should send my mother's overbaked biscuits to Vietnam
to use as bombs, everyone laughed, so I did too,

imagining green plastic men squashed by Bisquik.
My cousin Nancy and I danced to her 45
of the Beatles' "Help." We sang *Help! I need somebody.*

*Help! Not just anybody* until we fell down laughing.
When I asked her why they needed help, she said,
"Do I have to spell it out for you?"

When my cousin Johnny came home in his navy uniform
with a boxful of lobsters, I thought everyone cried
because he'd gotten them so cheap. When he said,

"The peace sign's the footprint of the American Chicken,"
I repeated it for days. No one wanted to turn off the tv those years,
although my parents let me, when Nixon interrupted *All in the Family*,

turn the sound down. Nothing good would
happen for the next hour once he appeared,
and I knew that wasn't why my mother hated him.

After dinner, everyone smoked, played poker,
told jokes I didn't get so I went out on the screened-in back porch
and listened to crickets fidget all over the dark lawn.

When the occasional curse exploded inside, I said it softly to myself
because it made everyone laugh. If they kept drinking, I might be forgotten,
get to watch the small brown spiders lay out their traps in the bushes

near the kitchen windows where moths banged, soft and dumb.
The way the spiders ran in for the kill stopped my breath.
One night, I heard my mother say she'd put

my older brother in the trunk and drive him to Canada
if it came to that. I thought she meant she liked me better, and,
because I wanted his bigger room, I thought, "Good."

## Why They Drank

They often smoked too, which made my eyes hurt. But it stopped their fingers twitching. Things were not so much falling apart as coming together into something new they could not hold. My father woke up in the early darkness and drank black coffee in it. My mother sometimes went to sleep fearing for her life. We didn't have leashes for the dogs normally, only when we went to the free rabies clinics where we talked with other people we knew. We were supposed to be rich. My father wanted to be richer because he didn't know how to be happier. My mother thought you made yourself rich by working with what you had and being careful. My father was beer until whiskey. My mother was vodka, although I thought most of my life it was gin. It seemed more ladylike. We took my grandmother Four Roses to say we loved her when she was unleashed. Nobody knew what to do with their war-selves after the war stopped. No one likes feeling small. My father liked taking orders but not from my mother. I couldn't breathe when my father sat me on his lap so I could tell him that I loved him like he told me to tell him. My mother drank hers as cold as she could I learned just before she died. There was always land for the dogs to run away into. Only one of them died because of a car. House after house didn't fix anything. I just kept being given bigger rooms to be afraid in. The dogs gradually all learned to sleep wherever I was.

## Lightning Mother

What if we
could be freed
from fear?
Not crashed.
The sound of it
flies after.  After
each stroke,
the strike (pale
pink, not white!)
curtaining the clouds
towns away, we
count seconds, divide
by—was it five?—
to get the miles right.
After the sun-hot
fever-forks vein
the miles of sky,
scorch its seams
until heaven heaves.
The windows rattle
around us on our
deep, safe porch.
Green rain arriving
fries the sidewalks
cracked by tree-roots
rising, more broken
mothers' backs laughing
children leap or try.
A good one, she says.
Nervousness cracks into
laughter, not after
but as another
wild thread
connects: she

could be
taken next by
those volts both
traintrack and engine,
to burn through hair
to tennis shoe, wedding
ring to finger forever.
It might be today
the needle spins
in the compass, grumbling,
the pocket knife closes
on a too slow finger,
the candle smells the gas
and reaches. My father's
getting drunk else-
where. There:
a thunderclap before
we think to count.  Moves
ice cubes melting in
my lemonade, squeezed
in anticipation of a break
like this in the weather.
The glass breaks into sweat.
We gasp and clap together.

Lines Near Midnight

The house is dark, the street nearly empty.
The clock goes on ticking dents in the silence,
the slow leak of time's liquids onto
the mantle. The dog sighs and slumps
on the floor. In the sink, a dish drips.

What did I do all day, I ask myself.
Days evaporate like newsprint in a fire.
I don't even have a scrap of an idea
what I had for dinner. There's a boat
with my name on it somewhere floating

off into deeper and deeper water.
I don't know whose hand is on the tiller.
I don't know what to do either with all
the depth I keep thinking I must be in now,
whether I'm rowing myself or just a shadow.

## Lines at the Winter Solstice

This darkness needs a praise song to survive it.
A song remembering what's inside each egg.
The before and after. How much is spent
gratefully in darkness, asleep, alone.

How much the winter dark repairs us
with pure listening. Consoles us with keys
and doors, intensities of blankets and bedrooms.
We wake early in it, step alone into

our showers' warm, dark hushes. Into such
simplicities of soap, shocked by our own touch.
Our own names wander off in a distant field.

A song for what's in closets all around us
where old clothes and new ones can't be told apart,
which attended funerals, which weddings.

Last Things

The sound of things
falling like wings

that are leaves losing
their last grips,

lost lips,
this first winter

without my mother,
loosed ships

the color of butter.

## Tick

Goes the ice in the thick river. Goes the worried
moon in the whispering window all night.
The dark comes down like a brick onto bones.
A song begins to stick in the quickness.

The morning takes its time tucking in its shirt,
pulling its new socks up. The clock tocks
on the black mantle next to the picture
of the Buddha and the six white candles

we've let melt down into puddles. We'll pick
the nearly wax-drowned wicks back to light
when we come home from work. The house creaks

just before the furnace kicks on. I keep
thinking certain things that prick like a sickness.
The trick's not to fixate. Let the faucets drip.

# The North

*for Galway Kinnell*

Far enough north and you can read
light written on ice, hear
whispers miles away, forget fire's
name. You blink back so many red veils

so often they stop being blood. The fur
of your parka becomes indistinguishable
from your own hair. When your compass
comes undone, its arrows turning

unsure, a quiver, then a blur,
you're at the end of the world where
the self is just one more minor flag.
There, you build a place in the snow

where you sleep until a roar
rises and blows out the fire.
Rises out of you, out of the endless,
restless miles, it doesn't matter.

## From The Book of Durations

Mother, I spent the first anniversary
of your last birthday in a strange man's arms.
You wouldn't want me to say that.

When I said gay and you said no, don't be.
When I said gay and you cried, afraid
I'd be killed by other people's anger.

It's hard to say the date was a coincidence or not.
I smelled his body right down to the root.
You wouldn't want me to say that

either. You taught me not to move suddenly
among predators, to assume anyone
anywhere could break open with hate.

We lived there once together, in that state.
When we escaped, we said never again. I kissed his feet.
You wouldn't want me to say that.

Maybe that isn't true. You also wanted me to be happy.
I can only speak about what you said, not what you meant
or thought to mean. I miss you. I'm not sorry.
I loved the way his hands erased your dead body.

MotherBird

Mockingbird, watched wings will not,
will not. If a cat, whistle like that,
far above the balcony among the ivy
creeping, until the cat below goes
still, looks up, its dream broken, leaves.

*Look at that*, my mother laughed,
cleaner of houses, valedictorian of
her class. *Free at last*, she clapped,
from man and landscape, old
cheerleader. *I love that bird.*

In her new place. Flies higher
among the complex power
and telephone wires, now's
a rusty hinge, suddenly
skylark, car alarm, dog bark.

Whatever it takes, what strange sing:
scrub iron dust empty mop
fold vacuum rearrange and get paid
for it at last. Even sell the ring,
old housewife. No one watching anymore.

Lines after Waking

I wake up now sometimes thinking I hear
things falling, a crash of metal boxes, a
heavy table collapsing, a window being
smashed into shark's teeth, moonlight, violence,

and I listen at first for the black dog
who is our best defense against robbery,
who's always burning to unleash his wolf
if the least touch lights upon a doorknob,

at the smallest whisper in the alley,
a tiny ping of metal on the backyard fence
as of strangers climbing over in the dark;
still, even if there's no sound from him of

anything wrong, I can't help but get up
and go down to see it's nothing again,
some sand in the ear where love used to whisper,
some contents shifting as during a flight.

Begin (river)

The river has returned to blue
after weeks of flooding
turned it brown. Falling
down, toward the Gulf,
one long thread from
the interior, it shines;
it hums in the dark, a work.
Sycamores on the bank soak
it up. Blackberries. Poison ivy
on the trunks. I think Lord
sometimes. I think Luck.
The dog thinks Door and
jumps into it like a key.

Fable

There was an apple tree I climbed into when I began to practice running away. It was the easiest one to hide in and close to the house so I could just lie if I got caught. Pretending nothing was happening was part of the plan. The apple tree was still bearing fruit. I might spend my days counting apples and listening to my parents yelling at each other about sacrifice.

When that didn't work, I hid inside a bush where I'd seen birds gathering, whole flocks of sparrows digging furrows in the dust underneath. When it started to rain, I looked up through its leaves at the sky coming down. I might stay here forever I thought, if I'd brought my good coat.

After that, they kept their eyes open for more little escapades. I couldn't stay underwater long enough, it turned out. And in the inch of air under the dock lived spiders rolling up balls of eggs I might breathe in. Nothing in the cattails but the sounds of herons flapping their outrage, the sky too empty, the floor too thin. Now and then a pike swam by with his bloody eyes, smiling.

Out at the farthest remove, near the sand cliffs where swifts flew in and out of burrowed holes, squadrons of emerald jets under each step, I finally sat down. A black snake ate something stupid nearby, flickered, and left. I thought: well, at least that will keep my father away. You might make soup out of burdocks and dandelions, they'd said. They all told me stories about whole families living off thimbles of snow and mushrooms under the bed during the Depression. I thought I could live there.

Until, far off my mother wept my most complicated name. I heard it damage the roses, the long grasses, the slim sumacs, which had appeared to reclaim what they could. The young saplings around me, which had been filling up with so much applause, stilled.

And without thinking, I was already answering, yes, yes, yes, of course, of course, hating how fast I returned.

Early Morning Rain

As long as I'm inside, the rain falling outside has a beautiful sound.

Even though my neighbor's car was stolen, and she has cancer or has had cancer, and now the street has an absence in it, like a missing tooth.

Even though I am tired of addressing you, of poems that address you and you and you.

Outside, the rain taps out its codes. Inside? it goes. Inside? inside?

In a minute I will get up from typing and get in the shower. So I can go out into the rain.

Why her car, I wonder. It was old. It had a support ovarian cancer research ribbon on it. It was nowhere near as interesting as the newer cars, including mine.

And only two more payments, she laughed, when she asked me if I'd heard anything that night.

No, and I'm so sorry I said, something I'd been waiting to say to her since I'd seen the ribbon on her trunk, since she'd begun losing so much weight.

You have nothing to do with it.

When I woke up last night, hearing voices, I checked that my own car was still there. Just the men in the halfway house across the street laughing as if no one else could sleep. *You fucker, you son of a bitch, you jackass.*

Someone else has already begun parking in the place where she used to park her car.

I was putting in a new bulb in my front door light. The old one had blown its dome off. I'd been concerned how a house without a light would look.

The straight lines of the rain are part of its beauty. How the rain sounds like someone driving away. The end of a vinyl record.

How it keeps all human voices off the street. Only you would sing about that.

Begin (root song)

The dirt is good
    enough, a kiss,
a hair of earth,
    flecked with minerals
whose thoughts bite
    with what's almost light
hissing where each
    chemical edge
unlocks the door
    to the long stairways
to the dead where
    you've had your ear
pressed so long
    waiting for a word.

## Lines Where Something Was Supposed To Be

I can feel where the nouns ought to be most days.
But often now I'm coming up short
when I go to grab that thing which one needs when one
needs to open a door in a conversation and cannot
find its name. My fingers flipper the air where
I know something should be solid, sayable,
and simply isn't. *The door thing. The thing you turn.*
*The thing, you know, you can lock and unlock.*
*The thing, oh my god, you can jiggle, you can try.*
Helpful, a friend will say, *oh you mean ----,*
and it will burst out of me with relief, the word,
the word, the word, I say over and over,
like the name of a lost child returned.
At least you knew it was lost, friends will say,
meaning I'm not that bad yet, I'm not one of those
whose language is really going, whose memory
is leaking away in some home full of strangers in white.
Not yet is what I hear, my hand on the *knob*. Not yet.

Begin (rain)

Its threads among the roots in a world without color.
It's the way the dead pass notes to one another.

Pomegranate 2

Once winter darkness fell, I cut into it.
I was hungry and it was what I had except
a kind of sadness from all day doing nothing
to help myself or save the world. The knife
was sharp enough to cut clean through the thin
hide of it and I knew how to lift its lid
where a flower'd been, where red lips pursed
in a kiss, a whisper, a last lost breath;
after which, inside, the seed rows grew
and rose and swelled like garnets, like bees, each
bearing the weight of an endless sweetness.
It took an hour off my hands to free each one.
The television flared with advertisements against listening.
The clock repeated itself like a priest.

Talking to the Dead

This time it was Irene whom I hadn't known well
but always wanted to, a poet-teacher, red-haired
and casual, a tough mountain-woman who died,
like my mother, of cancer. She appeared inside
another dream in which I was running from a monster,
a sky-filling kind of danger, like Godzilla. She'd been
doing errands when I saw her and followed her home.
The problem was I couldn't remember the name
of someone I thought she also knew, not Pat,
not Maggie, not RJ or Aaron, it was a woman but
not X or Y. Meanwhile Irene went on making tea
around me, waiting out my inability which never
resolved itself. Maybe it was the fear of forgetting
she was waiting out in her practical and kind way,
busying herself around me until I woke finally
to the sound of the wind pushing a can down the street.
Woke up in a sweat, the world having warmed up
too much for the comforter I was under. Woke up
alone, having snored my poor husband into the other room
again, whose own mother we feared was facing
a hard diagnosis. I lay there listening to the fan whir
that helps him get to sleep every night, that grinds
and soothes and smooths his iceberg thoughts. I am old,
I think for the thousandth time, and he's young, un-
used to dream-talking with the Dead, without a cast
of kitchens yet to imagine, still too new to life
to even know how good it felt to have had Irene
there buzzing around as I went on with name after name
until I came finally to a nothing, a namelessness
inside which I was sure there was someone lost to me
and I felt some urge to recover. The monster of the dream
had stopped mattering a long time ago. The whole world

might be burning but I wanted a single name back.
The tin can outside went on clattering down the street
like a man trying to remember something he saw once
maybe thirty years ago, maybe said two sentences to.
Something like a storm was swelling the sky with wind
but so far nothing was falling that I could hear,
that I could say the name of.

Varieties of Green and Distance

Up here, in this rented house, in these haunted mountains,
the sunrise rolls over the ridges like a slow wave;

it takes its time, rustling the super-saturated spaces
where warble, where caw, where nearly machine perfect

twittering in the trees nearby mean something I think
I can translate as excitement, business. A lone crow

paddles out into it, toward what is becoming now
a giant tide of pure sunlight, a falling redwood of

radiant energy, the keel of a gigantic ship bringing
what—Empire? Salvation? Humility? Do we know?

Near the end of her life my mother called me to say
*Look up tonight,* at a strange conjunction of Venus and Mars

and the Moon she'd never seen before. It was something,
even then, to hear. When she'd gotten rid of so much

she didn't think she'd need, there was still this surprise.
The one crow's disappeared into the rising surf of sunrise.

When the light reaches me, I stop asking where.

## Laughter Among Friends

One of us has something wrong. One of us is guilty. One is afraid in his silence he's losing it. One of us has an old dog. One of us has a puppy the size of a boy. One of us might not be herself anymore. But enough of that. Who knows anything? Anyway, we were playing cards and one of us squeaked instead of spoke and another of us picked up the squeak and there it went. We lose it, a bonfire of roses. A jungle of applications, medications, sign heres. One of us hasn't been kissed in years. He lets go of the blood balloon he's been holding onto. It floats away like a cake in a boat. We pound the table like a hull. We were playing cards for something to do. One of us is probably still drunk. One is losing his mother. Another has a father who might as well still be alive. About the self-worth. About the body doesn't breathe as well as it used to. The squeak blooms, roars, transforms drowning into a craft. A strangle released at last. The leap made into the leopard. Each of us runs toward it the way a dog will run toward the sound of a fight. To see what will happen maybe. To nip at a stray leg flashing. What the fuck do we care? The moon banging on the glass in oh my gods, in Jesuses. Each of us trying to stand. One of us lets himself fall down hard. One of us bends herself over a chair. Oh my god it's just cards. Anyway we hurt, we hurt, we hurt. All smashed up on the floor, holding ourselves together. The dogs watch us like we're wrecked. To see if any food falls out.

Advice

There is nothing saying you have to wait.
Waiting is for coins in a pocket. It's for
things like irons and teaspoons. A gate

waits to be pushed or opened, a crate
to be filled with objects to save. However,
there is nothing saying you have to wait.

You could begin right now. It's always too late
or too early. You don't have to be able to drive a car.
Things like The Silver, those photos you love to hate,

you can leave them. You can leave the state
if you want. You don't even need a literal door.
There is nothing saying you have to wait.

Leave the dust alone. You don't even need light.
You've been all coiled up, unpredictable as the weather.
The thing about time is it never feels right.

You have to begin somewhere. Forget the date
and the cost of everything but your hunger.
There is nothing saying you have to wait
if things are wrong. Nor is moving always flight.

## Even in Pittsburgh

Just before we go to bed every night,
the sound of the dog lapping the water
out of his big silver dish in the kitchen
becomes a body hauling itself
onto a strange shore after a long night swimming
in the ocean, a shipwreck's sunken
weight behind him somewhere darkly
grinding sand into further dissolves.

I take the black leash from the top
of the refrigerator and clip it to his collar.
We walk down to the end of the block, a lot
abandoned to weeds where he pees
a long thoughtful moment. Tonight's full moon,
earth's old inoculation scar, our constant
Otherwise floods the street. It's a light with weight.
It makes the sound of someone else in the room.

At home, I turn off the lights, knowing
the house all the way through, preferring it
that way sometimes. Turn all the locks.
The dog follows me with a glow-in-the-dark ball
in his mouth. It's like a joke he's been waiting
to spring on me and which I can't figure out
until I hear his tail wagging him up the stairs.
I rub my eyes like a sailor signing a contract.
We strip to skin and fur, climb back into the sails.

## The Questions

An orange, a wreckage, a circumference
ruined by hands. Torn apart to taste it.
A crown of discards now, an instance,
today's hunger. There's always something
said my grandmother who used to hand me
her big tin of buttons to find a pair she could use.
It rattled like a rainstorm in my hands, slid
around, a box of scales, while she pedaled
the black iron treadle of her Singer into hidden seams.
Out of nothing she'd shake out a sleeve, a shirt.
I'd sift fingers through a gravel of buttons, their
fabric, plastic, bone and shell. Some I'd hold up
to admire better, to consider their effects in light.
It's the little things, she said, that matter. But
she knew how to do the big things too--could bake
cakes out of drawer dust, out of coffee grounds.
Find the tenderest meat in the cheapest round.
We all knew she'd gotten us through the Depression.
With my grandfather who could twist metal
into any shape, who could grind a diamond back
into useful coal, recatch the time in a long-stopped watch.
Even my angry father could tear up a floor to lay
a better balance in it. I got some of my mother's math,
thank God but lost the family whose taxes it did.
I should have paid attention I suppose, but each
had his or her own beauty I didn't want to interrupt
with questions. How to make things out of nothing.
How to throw nothing away.

Driving

My brother reminds me of the time my father slammed a beautiful new car we owned into reverse and destroyed the transmission. He was drunk like always. We are ourselves driving back from a trip to the ocean where we scattered our mother's ashes into the crashing curls of the Atlantic Ocean. My brother needs to stop every hour or so to pee or to eat something. Isn't it true, I say, that once our father drove into a cowfield and fell asleep? My brother laughs, yes, he rolled it over. He woke up and crawled out. All that night we hoped he wouldn't come home, that maybe this time he'd die. Didn't we pray for that every night, I say. I'm the age my mother was when she divorced him finally and we moved away from the terror of his tires on the gravel after midnight. All the rest of Pennsylvania for us to get through, fog in the mountains, drizzles of rain, the weaving of semis on the interstate, neither of us fathers ourselves. We take turns driving while the other one snores in the passenger seat in a very familiar way.

## When We Disappeared

Once upon a time, my mother and I pulled off the road, walked into a field of golden grass and weeds, and disappeared. Maybe I was six, maybe ten. We took a bucket of chicken we'd bought in Geneva, either at KFC or at its local knock-off, The Red Barn. I don't remember if we had a blanket, if we had anything to drink, if there were biscuits or napkins or sporks. I don't remember what we talked about or might have talked about. I don't remember why we were on the road, although I do remember it was a country road, a road that wound through and around farmhouses, stables, fields. It was a day of bright light and tall weeds, so late summer or early fall.

We were probably playing hooky from our lives. My mother loved to drive. It rested her mind to be moving. When she was upset or bored or depressed, she drove, sometimes inventing errands she had to run, things I needed for school, groceries that could only be found a half hour away, books in distant libraries she wanted to read. There were a million excuses, but she liked the ones that sounded practical, things she wouldn't have to explain to anyone, or more likely, since to my knowledge nobody asked, she didn't want to explain her restlessness to herself.

Since I was too young to leave at home, she usually took me along. Maybe twice a year she'd write me a note to skip school and we'd go to the racetrack and bet on the horses. My school guidance counselor was usually there, and he and she would nod politely, so I never got in trouble. On weekends, if I was growing bored and sulky, she'd suggest I go along with her on errands. "To blow the stink off" is how she phrased it.

We'd drive out of town, windows down, out past the houses and names we knew, out past the big fields of endless corn or wheat or grass whose only inhabitants we could see were big hawks perched on fence posts or telephone poles, out and out until I'd forgotten the point of our driving, why we were going and where. Often, she'd stop at a barn or garage sale, and while I tried to vanish with embarrassment, she'd get out and look at what other people were willing to part with, have a little conversation with a few strangers, and then get back in, usually empty-handed, and drive on.

We'd meander like that until we got to where she'd said we were going. Usually, it would be a place where we could return to the world of doing things. Maybe that's why, when she pulled over that one day, it surprised me enough to make a memory of golden grasses and bright but not hot light. I loved my mother, and I often loved having her all to myself on those drives. I've never forgotten that picnic with her, that time we both disappeared from our lives. We left the car behind on the side of the road. We found a place among what I imagine now as the buzz and pulse of late summer, early fall insects. We opened our bucket of golden hot crunchy chicken and buttery joy, and we let the world absorb us. For ten minutes, an hour, how long, I don't know. It doesn't matter to me now. How long does a poem by Rilke take to read? How long does it take a horse to run around a track? No time at all.

## Like Grass

If something in your name is like grass,
there's an urge to mow it down. If it
sways in any breeze, if it sounds like
a half-laugh

in the middle of an argument between
whether you're a son or a daughter,
some weed to be dealt with sooner
or later in the evening when

the wind through the window makes
a sheet of loose leaf
flap. You look up as if called.
If something in your name

is also like a sigh at again not
being missed.  You go unnoticed
among the blades in the lawn, sheets
softened first then folded, the cats

in the alley. Just at the edge of a cuff.
A bit of last love to spend said
your mother. The name came
out of nowhere. It was a last gasp.

"In my craft…"

Exercised at first to hold her
When I knew that time was dying
And nothing would be left, only
With memory's dim light to trust,
I described, sometimes beside her
Not wanting to say anything
Or with a pen ruin laughter
On the altar of sullen art
But still needing to keep some things
Of her life near me forever

Not to have everything fall away
From my own life I thought might die
On her last breath; and here I am
Nor would she have wanted me to
With all her training not survive
But knew I had to write it down,
Round her edges, sharpen her tongue,
Who knew me from the beginning
Nor would ever leave me alone.

## Acknowledgements

Many thanks to the journals and editors who published these poems, sometimes in slightly different forms:

*5 a.m.:* Driving Lesson; What We Knew
*About Place:* Late Stage
*Assaracus:* After Grief
*The Portable Boog Reader #7:* The Purple Robe
*Chelsea Station:* From the Book of Durations
*Coal Hill Review:* Early Morning Rain; The North
*Field:* Even in Pittsburgh
*The Fourth River Review:* To Spring; The Allegheny River; Kissing the River
*Georgia Review:* Lines at the Winter Solstice
*Good Men's Project:* Advice
*Mead:* Pomegranate
*Mid-American Review:* At the End of the Street
*Missouri Review:* What Is to be Done With Silence
*Pittsburgh Poetry Review:* On the Black Dog; Being Met
*Pittsburgh Post-Gazette:* Lines Where Something was Supposed to Be
*Prairie Schooner:* Small Rain
*storySouth:* The End of Summer
*Tupelo Quarterly:* The Visit; The Shit; Water
*Water-Stone Review:* Driving

"The Black Dog in the Middle of the Night" appeared in *The Familiar Wild*, Sundress Publications, 2020. Thank you to editors Rachel Mennies and Ruth Awad for including it.

"The Things" appeared as a broadside for the 2013 PA Center for the Book, Penn State University.

Lines from "Late Stage" are from David Hinton's translation of Liu Tsung-Yüan's "In Reply to Chia P'eng of the Mountains, Sent Upon Seeing That the Pine He Planted Outside My Office Has Begun to Prosper" in *Mountain Home* (New Directions, 2005).

"In My Craft..." uses the first words of Dylan Thomas' poem "In my craft or sullen art" as its skeleton.

## Personal Acknowledgements:

I would like to thank a number of people who read drafts of these poems and/or supported me during the writing of this book, most especially Geeta Kothari, Noah Stetzer, Jan Freeman, Toi Derricotte, and Lynn Emanuel.

I also especially want to thank The Grind, without which many of these poems simply wouldn't have been written. Thanks to Jenny Johnson, who generously invited me to it, and to the indefatigable Ross White who keeps it going. And to the many Grinders who inspired and kept me accountable.

Deep bows of appreciation to Eileen Cleary for her faith in this book and to Martha McCollough for her attention to its design.

## ABOUT THE AUTHOR

Jeff Oaks' debut book of poetry, *Little What*, was published by Lily Poetry Review Books in September 2019. A recipient of three Pennsylvania Council of the Arts fellowships, Oaks has published poems in a number of literary magazines, most recently in *Field, Georgia Review, Missouri Review, Superstition Review,* and *Tupelo Quarterly.* His work has appeared in the anthologies *The Familiar Wild: on Dogs and Poetry, Brief Encounters: A Collection of Contemporary Nonfiction,* and *My Diva: 65 Gay Men on the Women Who Inspire Them.* He teaches writing at the University of Pittsburgh.

www.ingramcontent.com/pod-product-compliance
Lightning Source LLC
Chambersburg PA
CBHW072207100526
**44589CB00015B/2416**